In the Beginning God
Created the Heavens...
The Planets

The Bible Tells Me So Press

In the Beginning God Created the Heavens…
The Planets

A children's book produced by
The Bible Tells Me So Press

Copyright © 2019
The Bible Tells Me So Corporation

All rights reserved. No part of this book, neither text nor illustrations, may be reproduced or stored in any form or by any electronic or mechanical means without permission in writing by the publisher.

PUBLISHED BY
THE BIBLE TELLS ME SO CORPORATION
2111 W. CRESCENT AVE, SUITE C, ANAHEIM, CA 92801
WWW.THEBIBLETELLSMESO.COM

Images and elements of images
courtesy NASA/JPL-Caltech.

First Printing February, 2019

The earth is **very special** to God and very special to us.

How special is it?

Let's take a journey
to visit the other planets
in our solar system
to see how they compare
with the earth.

We will see
that God made the earth
to be the very best place
for us to live.

Our first stop will be
the closest planet to the sun.

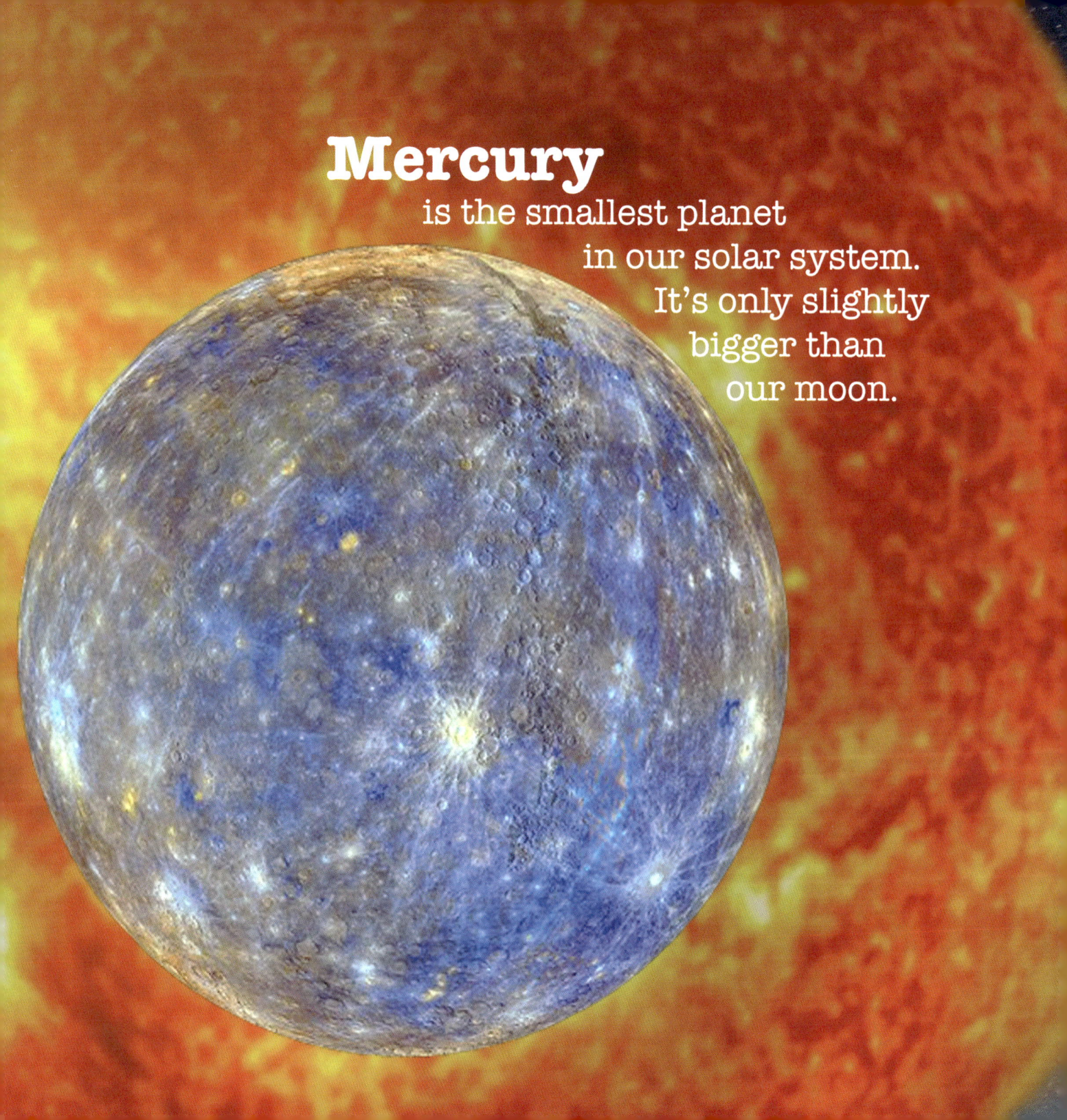

Mercury
is the smallest planet in our solar system. It's only slightly bigger than our moon.

Nothing can live on Mercury.

What little atmosphere there is on Mercury is **toxic**.

During the day, Mercury is hot enough to melt lead!

Then, at night it becomes super freezing. It has the most extreme temperature changes than any other planet.

Mercury is **not** the place for us!

Venus
is a very difficult and strange place.

It is
the hottest
of all the planets in our solar system.
It's even hotter that Mercury!

It has thousands of active volcanoes that make **rivers of lava**, that are longer than any river on the earth.

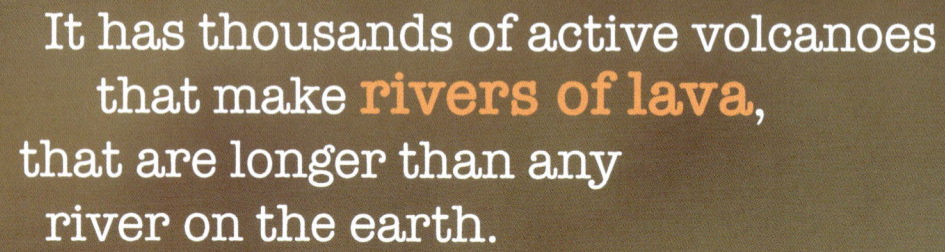

It would be **impossible** to live on Venus, not only because of the extreme heat, strong winds, and **toxic atmosphere**, but also because the thick clouds that cover the planet are made up of poisonous **acid!**

Venus is also **not** the place for us!

Let's go on to visit
Mars.

Mars also has very extreme weather.
The normal temperature
on Mars is very cold.

The thin atmosphere on Mars
is made up mainly of **poisonous gases**
which cannot protect it against
harmful rays from the sun.

Mars also has the largest volcano
of all the planets in the solar system.

If that's not bad enough, Mars has the biggest dust storms as well. They can cover the entire planet and last for months at a time!

Mars may be fine **for a robot** to roll around on for a while,

but Mars is **not** the place for us.

Jupiter
is the largest planet
in our solar system,
but it's not a solid planet.
It is made up almost
entirely of **toxic gases**.

Jupiter is also very cold
and also has large
and violent storms
that form quickly
and last a long time.

In fact, the big, red, swirling circle on Jupiter is a **huge** storm called the "Great Red Spot."

It has been going on for **over 150 years** and is twice the size of earth. That's a **big** storm!

Jupiter is **not** the place for us!

Saturn
is the planet with the beautiful rings.

But it also has **super-fast winds** and is very cold!

The rings around Saturn are not solid.
They are made of rocks, tiny pieces of dust, and ice.

Like Jupiter, Saturn is not a solid planet.
It's made of **toxic gases**,
making it impossible
to stand on,
much less
live on.

Saturn is **not** the place for us either!

Uranus

is another planet that is mostly
made up of **toxic gases** and
does not have a solid surface.

It is tilted on its side,
spins sideways,
and rotates in the opposite direction
of most of the other planets.

It's extremely cold, has strong winds, and is completely covered by thick blue clouds that are not only **toxic** but also smell like **rotten eggs!**

So there's no doubt that Uranus is **not** the place for us.

Neptune
is the furthest planet from the sun.

While Uranus is sometimes colder than Neptune,
on average, Neptune is the **coldest planet**
in the solar system.

Neptune also is not a solid planet.
It has a **toxic** atmosphere,
and it too has very violent storms, with
the fastest winds
in the solar system!

Neptune is
definitely not
the place for us either!

Now, let's come back and take a look at...

Earth!

God placed the earth at the **perfect distance** from the sun to give us **comfortable temperatures**.

He tilted it at **just the right angle** to give us **wonderful seasons**.

He caused it to spin at **just the right speed** to give us **perfect days**.

And God gave the earth a **beautiful** and **clear** atmosphere that protects us from the sun's harmful rays.

The earth is **the only planet** in the solar system that has **oxygen** and **liquid water**— **a lot of it!**

While scientists have not found
a trace of life on any
other planet,

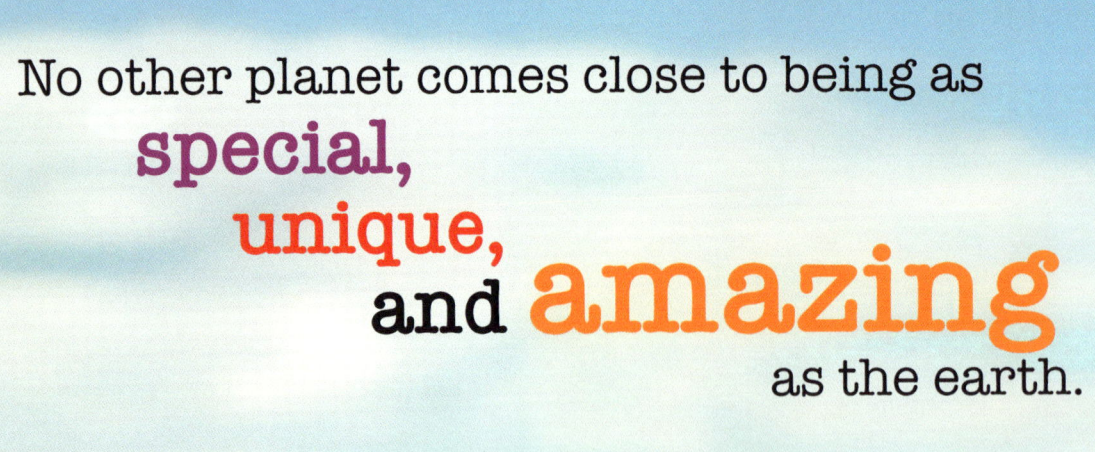

No other planet comes close to being as **special,** **unique,** and **amazing** as the earth.

God **purposely** made the earth this way for **you** and for **me**.

This
is the place for us!

Thank You Lord,
for the earth!

For thus says Jehovah...
Who formed the earth and made it...
to be inhabited..."

Isaiah 45:18

For more
books, videos, songs, and crafts
visit us online at
TheBibleTellsMeSo.com

Standing on the Bible and growing!

Printed in Great
Britain
by Amazon